To my mom, Eileen, my father, Frank, and my grandpa Frank,
who made my childhood so memorable. It was always an adventure
on our farm, with plenty of fun. Thank you.
—T. G.

To Mina's mom, Anna, to Grandma Trueman and Grandma Collins,
and to Tata Michèle, who all helped me get this done.
—M. T.

Text © 2009 by Tony Gemignani.
Illustrations © 2009 by Matthew Trueman.

Book design by Amy E. Achaibou.
Typeset in Antique3.
Additional text by June Eding.
The illustrations in this book were rendered in mixed media.
Manufactured in China.

Library of Congress Cataloging-in-Publication Data
Gemignani, Tony.
Tony and the pizza champions / by Tony Gemignani ; illustrated by Matthew Trueman.
p. cm.
"Additional text by June Eding"—Copyright p.
Summary: When Tossing Tony is invited to the World Pizza Championship in Italy, he
forms a team with Quick Ken, Strong Sean, Mighty Mike, Silly Siler, and Famous Joe,
along with a top secret, incredible routine for the competition. Includes a recipe for
pizza and instructions for tossing pizza dough.
ISBN 978-0-8118-6162-5
[1. Pizza—Fiction. 2. Contests—Fiction. 3. Cooperativeness—Fiction. 4. Italy—Fiction.] I.
Trueman, Matthew, ill. II. Title.
PZ7.G2848To 2009
[E]—dc22
2007048046

10 9 8 7 6 5 4 3 2 1

Chronicle Books LLC
680 Second Street, San Francisco, California 94107

www.chroniclekids.com

TONY AND THE PIZZA CHAMPIONS

BY **Tony Gemignani**

ILLUSTRATED BY **Matthew Trueman**

chronicle books · san francisco

Like lots of people all over the world, Tony loves pizza. But Tony doesn't just love *eating* pizza—he loves *tossing* it, too!

Tony is so good at tossing pizza dough that everyone calls him Tossing Tony.

Tony's friends love tossing pizza, too. Tony's friend Ken can do a move called the **WHIRLWIND.** He tosses so fast that his friends call him Quick Ken.

Tony and Ken work at the same pizzeria in California. One day, while Tony was practicing his tossing moves, Ken opened a letter that had come all the way from Italy.

Tony took one look at the letter and dropped his dough with a *splat*.

"Hold the anchovies!" Tony said. "This looks important!"

Dear Tony,

You and your team are cordially invited to attend the World Pizza Championship in Italy. You will compete against teams from around the world to see who can serve up the best pizza-tossing performance. Good luck!

—The World Pizza Judges

"The World Pizza Championship!" Tony cheered. "Let's go!"

"Yeah!" Ken said. "But wait—don't we need a whole team?"

"We do," said Tony. "So we're going to have to build the perfect team . . ."

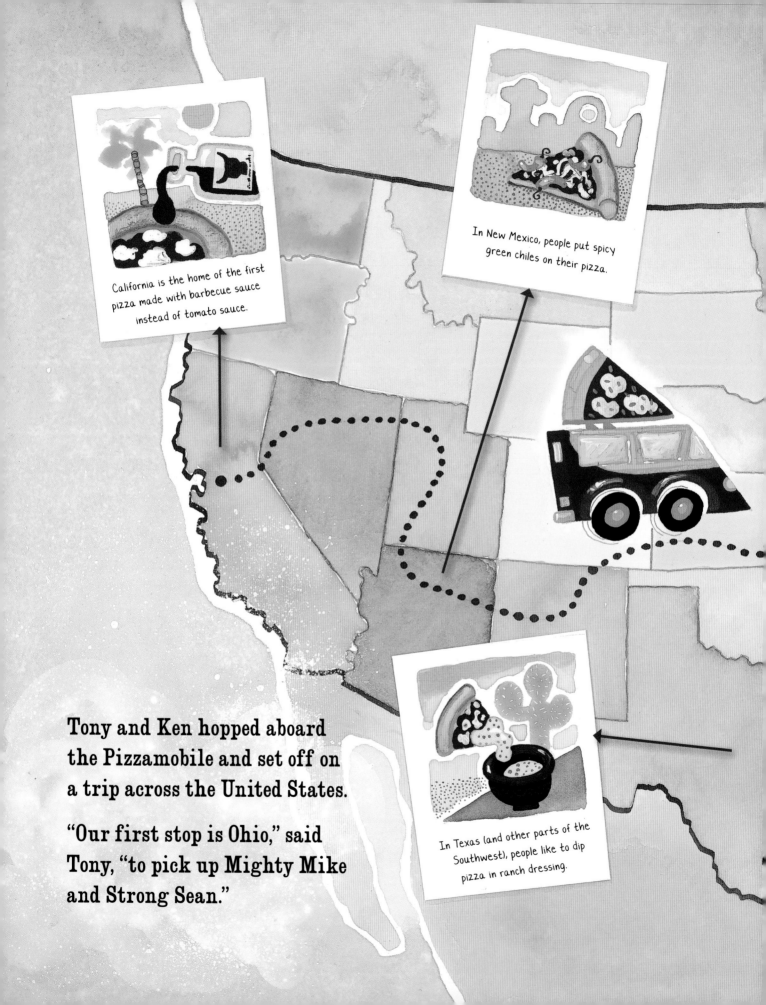

California is the home of the first pizza made with barbecue sauce instead of tomato sauce.

In New Mexico, people put spicy green chiles on their pizza.

In Texas (and other parts of the Southwest), people like to dip pizza in ranch dressing.

Tony and Ken hopped aboard the Pizzamobile and set off on a trip across the United States.

"Our first stop is Ohio," said Tony, "to pick up Mighty Mike and Strong Sean."

In Philadelphia, some people wrap pizza slices around cheesesteak sandwiches.

In Connecticut, restaurants serve pizza with clams on top.

In Rhode Island, you can order a pizza that's cooked on a grill, just like a hamburger.

The first pizzeria in the United States was opened in New York City in 1905.

In St. Louis, a mixture of white Cheddar, Swiss, and provolone cheese is popular instead of mozzarella.

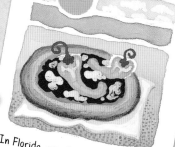

In Florida, people like to top their pizza with banana peppers (sweet peppers that are yellow, like bananas).

The Pizzamobile screeched to a halt in front of Sean's house. Someone was on the front lawn, spinning a huge circle of pizza dough. It was so big, you couldn't see who was tossing it!

"That's Strong Sean!" said Tony. "I'd recognize those shoes anywhere."

"But where's Mighty Mike?" asked Ken.

Suddenly, someone *else* emerged from underneath the spinning dough.

"Hey, guys, how can I help you?" asked Mike, rolling dough over his shoulders. That was Mike's favorite move: the **RAPID FIRE.**

Tony and Ken asked Mike and Sean if they would join their team.

"You bet your pizza dough!" said Mike and Sean together.

All four guys piled into the Pizzamobile and hit the road. It was a tight squeeze.

"It's a good thing I ordered an extra-large van," thought Tony.

The next stop was South Carolina, where Tony's friend Silly Siler had a pizza parlor. They arrived just in time for dinner. The place was packed! And where was Siler?

Just then, a young man burst out of the kitchen. He was tossing dough in each hand and riding a unicycle at the same time!

Happily, Siler agreed to join the team—as long as he could bring his unicycle.

MENU

WE DELIVER!

Mom's Favorite . . . . . Lg $16.99

Chicken

Lg $17.99

Lg $16.99

Lg $16.99

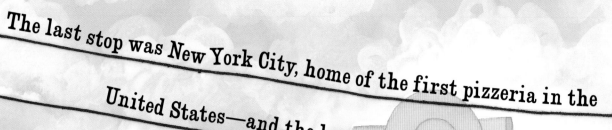

The last stop was New York City, home of the first pizzeria in the United States—and the home of Famous Joe. When the guys arrived in the city, Joe was ready to go.

"That's one of the things Famous Joe is famous for," said Tony. "He's got great timing!"

Famous Joe is also famous for doing the **SKY-HIGH.** He can toss dough high into the air, catch it on one arm, and roll it across his back to the other arm!

Now that the team was assembled, it was time to practice, practice, practice.

After hours of tossing, the guys were *really* tired. But it had been worth it: Now they had an absolutely unbelievable, totally incredible routine. It was so good that it was

TOP SECRET.

The next day, the team flew to Italy. They couldn't practice tossing dough on the plane, so instead they talked about all the different ways people eat pizza around the world.

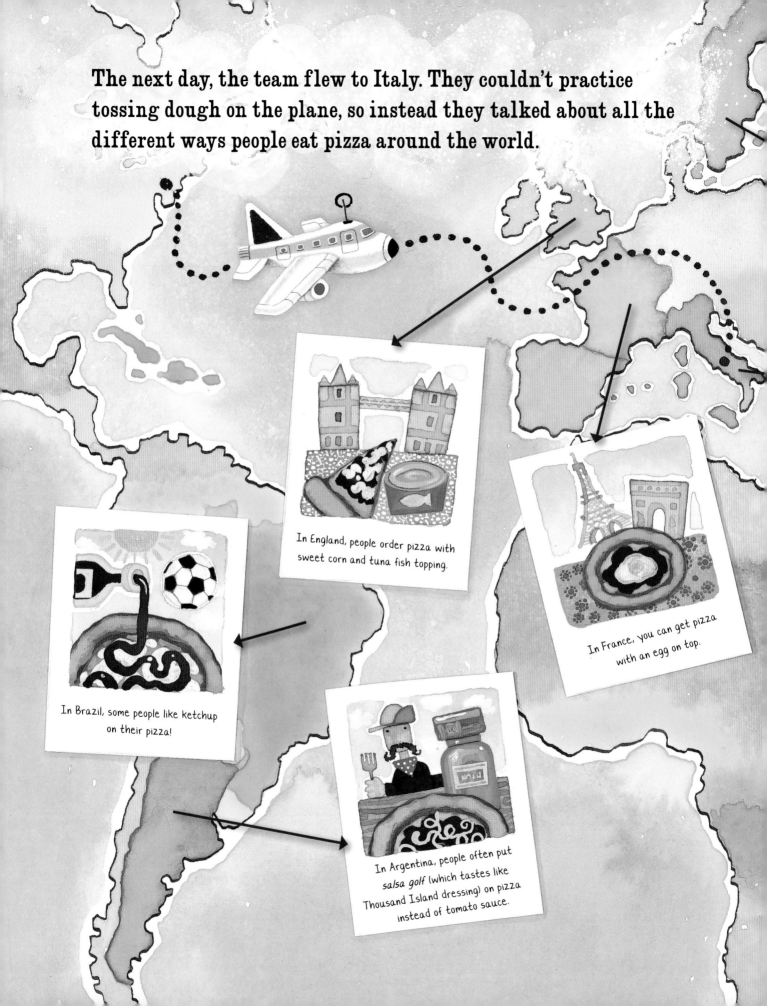

In England, people order pizza with sweet corn and tuna fish topping.

In France, you can get pizza with an egg on top.

In Brazil, some people like ketchup on their pizza!

In Argentina, people often put *salsa golf* (which tastes like Thousand Island dressing) on pizza instead of tomato sauce.

In Sweden, you can expect to get a side of coleslaw with your pizza.

In some parts of Italy, people put French fries on their pizza!

In Japan, you can order a pizza with mayonnaise, squid ink, or fish eggs on it!

Greetings from Italy!

Finally the big day was here—the day of the World Pizza Championship! When Tony and his team arrived at the competition, dough was flying as teams from around the world showed their skills.

The team from Japan tossed dough in a great circle: behind their backs, over their heads, between their legs, and onto their heads!

Next up was the Australian team. They formed a long line, and, one by one, tossed the dough in the air, jumped over the person in front of them, and caught the dough before it fell! They looked like a mob of pizza-tossing kangaroos!

The team from Brazil tossed dough around and around in a big whirling circle that looked like a pizza tornado!

The team from Italy did headstands and backflips so fast that their costumes were just a blur of color! Pizza dough flew back and forth in arcs high above them.

At last, it was time for Tony's team to perform. They all wiped the sweat from their brows and tried not to think about the competition.

"Teamwork," they said to themselves. "It's all about teamwork."

First Ken stepped forward, spinning around and tossing dough behind his back so quickly that he looked like a twirling ice-skater.

Then Mike joined him, rolling dough across his shoulders as fast as he could. Then Famous Joe joined in, tossing dough way up high and catching it on his shoulders. Tony was in the very front, performing his best move: the **DOUBLE TROUBLE.**

Then Sean appeared. He lined up with Mike and Ken,

and they lifted Joe and Tony onto their shoulders.

The only one missing was Silly Siler.

Where was he?

From off in the distance, a shape came speeding toward them. It was Silly Siler on his unicycle! He was juggling two circles of dough as he rode closer and closer.

Suddenly, Siler
jumped off the unicycle
and leaped high up into the
air. He landed right on Joe and
Tony's shoulders! Everyone held
steady. They had done it!
They had formed . . .

"Bravo!" said the judge as he presented the team with gold medals. "Tossing Tony, you and your team are now the

WORLD PIZZA CHAMPIONS!"

As the crowd cheered, Tony turned to his team and said, "Just like the perfect pizza, our team had all the right ingredients!"

Meet the *real* World Pizza Champions! Tony and his team have won more than ten world pizza championship titles.

KEN   SILER   TONY   JOE   MIKE

MIKE

SEAN

JOE

TONY

SILER

KEN

Here's how to make your very own pizza from scratch. Just plan ahead because the dough takes 10 hours to rise!

Tossing Tony's Pizza Dough
(makes enough dough for two 14-inch pizzas)

Ingredients:

1 cup (240 ml) lukewarm water
1 package (2¼ teaspoons, 10 ml) active dry yeast
1 cup (240 ml) ice-cold water
1 tablespoon (15 ml) sugar
1 tablespoon (15 ml) salt, or 1½ tablespoons (23 ml) kosher salt
5¼ cups (1 l) unbleached bread flour, plus flour for work surface
2 tablespoons (30 ml) olive oil

Directions:

1. Fill a small bowl with the lukewarm water, and use a fork to stir in the yeast. Set aside until the yeast dissolves, about 5 minutes.

2. In another small bowl, combine the cold water, sugar, and salt until the sugar and salt are dissolved.

3. Make the dough by hand or with a mixer.
   To make the dough by hand:
   - Place flour in a large bowl.
   - Make a well in the center of the flour, and stir in the yeast mixture and the cold-water mixture.
   - Using a wooden spoon, mix the ingredients together, incorporating as much of the flour as possible. Then add olive oil and continue mixing.
   - Turn the dough out onto a lightly floured work surface, and knead until it's soft and elastic, about 10 to 12 minutes. It is okay if it's a little sticky, but it shouldn't stick to your hands.

To make the dough using a mixer (adult help needed):
   - Fit a heavy-duty stand mixer with the dough-hook attachment.
   - Place the flour in the mixer bowl.
   - Add the yeast mixture and the cold-water mixture, and mix on low speed for about 4 minutes, or until the flour is incorporated and the dough forms a ball. Let it rest for 2 minutes.
   - Add olive oil and mix on low speed for about 6 minutes, or until the dough is smooth and not sticky.

· Turn the dough out onto a lightly floured surface, and knead for about 2 minutes.

4. Cut the dough in half to form two equal portions.

5. Pick up one portion of your dough and begin shaping it into a ball by folding in the edges.

6. Turn your dough over and close up the open parts by pinching the dough together.

7. Repeat steps 5 and 6 with the second portion.

8. Place each piece of dough in a plastic bag with a zip closure. There should be enough empty space in the bag to allow room for the dough to double in size, because it's going to rise (a lot!). Squeeze out all the air and seal each bag.

9. Refrigerate the dough for at least 10 hours, or up to 2 days. Remove from the refrigerator 1 hour before using, and let the dough warm up to room temperature.

Visit
WWW.CHRONICLEBOOKS.COM/
PIZZACHAMPS
to see videos of
Tony making and
tossing dough!

How to Toss Pizza Dough

→ **A NOTE FROM TONY:** I've been tossing pizza dough for a *long* time, but all my complicated tricks start with this basic toss. Go ahead and give it a whirl!

Get Ready

1. First, remove any jewelry, and wash your hands. Then sprinkle your work surface with flour.

2. Smash the dough with your hands to make a flat disk.

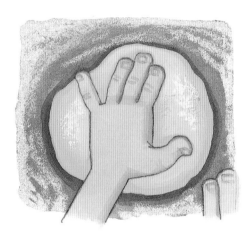

3. Using your hands or a rolling pin, stretch and shape the dough until it's a flat circle, about 8 to 10 inches (20 to 25 cm) across.

4. Place the dough in the palm of your right hand (if you're right-handed) or your left hand (if you're left-handed). Keep your fingers together, not spread out. Make a fist with your other hand, and support the rest of the dough with it (so it stays level and doesn't flop).

RIGHT-HANDED

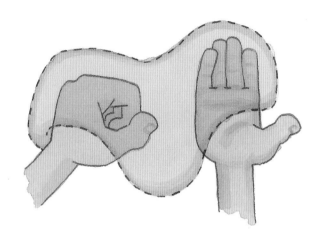

LEFT-HANDED

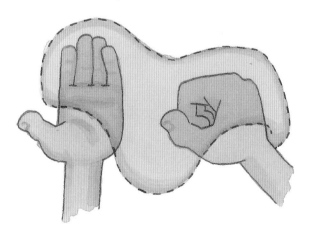

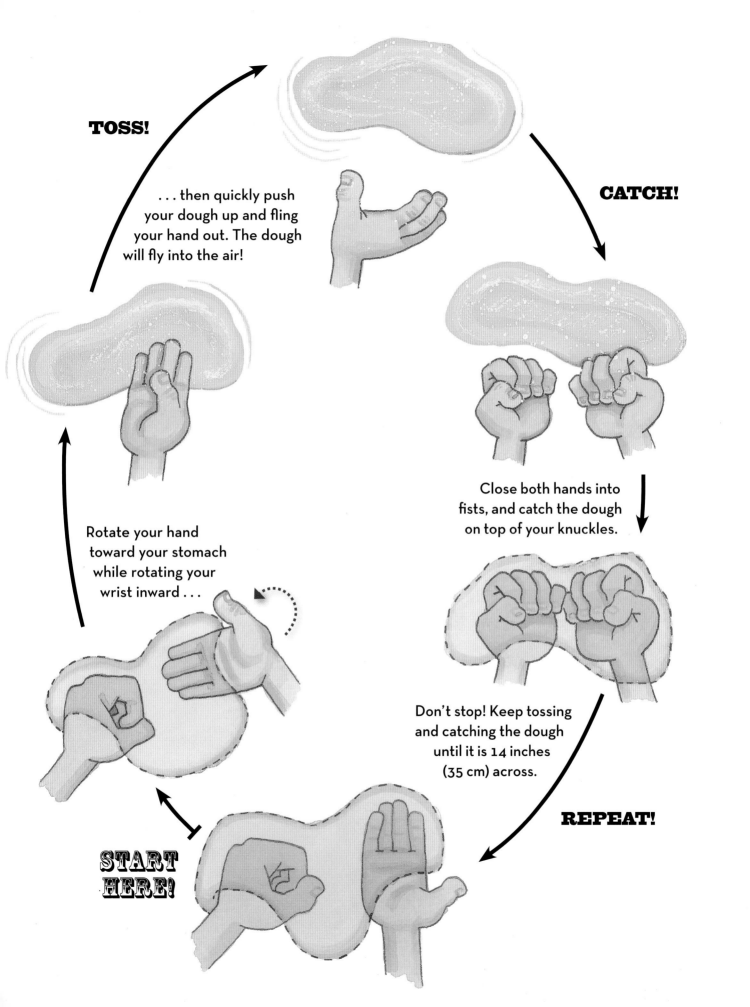

TOSS!

. . . then quickly push your dough up and fling your hand out. The dough will fly into the air!

CATCH!

Close both hands into fists, and catch the dough on top of your knuckles.

Rotate your hand toward your stomach while rotating your wrist inward . . .

Don't stop! Keep tossing and catching the dough until it is 14 inches (35 cm) across.

REPEAT!

START HERE!

The Big Cheese Pizza

→ **A NOTE FROM TONY:** Instead of store-bought tomato sauce, try my fast and delicious pizza sauce recipe. You'll find it at www.chroniclebooks.com/pizzachamps.

Ingredients:

1 portion Tossing Tony's Pizza Dough
Unbleached bread flour, for dusting
³/₄ cup (180 ml) tomato sauce
1¹/₂ cups (360 ml) shredded, 100% whole-milk mozzarella cheese

Equipment needed:

Pizza stone and pizza peel (available from cooking stores)
Rolling pin
Pizza cutter

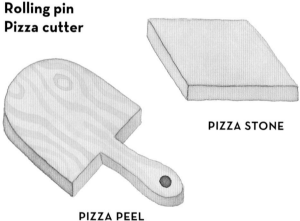

PIZZA STONE

PIZZA PEEL

Directions:

1. Position an oven rack on the second-lowest level in the oven, and place a pizza stone on the rack. Then preheat the oven to 500 degrees F (260 degrees C). Now that's HOT!

2. Toss one portion of dough (as described on the previous pages) until it is 14 inches in diameter.

3. Dust a pizza peel with flour. Carefully lay the dough onto the peel. Give the pizza peel a few shakes to be sure the dough is not sticking. (If your dough *is* sticking, try blowing underneath the pizza. Or gently pick up your pizza, and add some flour to the bottom.)

4. Now it's time for the sauce: Spread it evenly over the dough. Be sure to leave a 1-inch (2.5-cm) border around the edge for the crust.

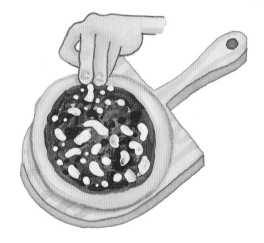

5. Here comes the cheese! Sprinkle the mozzarella all over your pizza.

6. See the Pizza Faces section for topping ideas.

7. Gently shake the pizza peel again to make sure your pizza is not sticking to it, and then have an adult place the pizza on the pizza stone in the VERY HOT oven. (If the dough is sticking, try the tricks from step 3.)

8. Your pie only needs to cook for 8 to 10 minutes, until the crust is golden brown.

9. YUM! Have an adult remove your pizza from the oven and place it on a cutting board. Give the pizza some time to cool (hot cheese burns!), and then have an adult slice it.

Then it's time for you to *mangi*—that's Italian for eat!

Pizza Faces

→ **A NOTE FROM TONY:** You can use different ingredients to make a pizza face, complete with ears, nose, eyes—even a bow tie! Keep in mind that the toppings will move around a bit as the pizza bakes. If you want to make sure things stay put, add the ingredients that can be eaten raw *after* the pizza comes out of the oven.

☑ **Eyes:**
- Black olives
- Pepperoni slices
- Sausage chunks

☑ **Lips:**
- Tomato slivers
- Pepperoni slivers
- Red bell pepper slivers

☑ **Hair:**
- Shredded Cheddar cheese
- Oregano sprinkles, or another spice
- Broccoli or spinach, chopped
- White onion slices

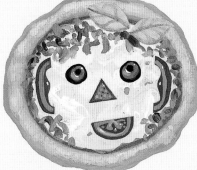
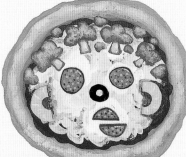

☑ **Bow for hair or bow tie:**
- 2 fresh basil leaves

☑ **Nose:**
- Pepperoni, cut into a triangle
- Tomato slice
- Black olive

☑ **Ears:**
- Bell pepper slices
- Pineapple slices
- Tomato slices

☑ **Freckles:**
- Black pepper or spice sprinkles